Recreating The 18th Century Powder Horn

By Scott & Cathy Sibley

Published in the United States by:

Track of the Wolf Inc.
18308 Joplin Street N.W.
Elk River, MN 55330-1173
www.trackofthewolf.com

Copyright © Track of the Wolf Inc. 2005

All rights reserved. Except for use in review, no part of this book may be reproduced or transmitted in any form or by any means, electronic or mechanical, including photocopying and recording, or by an information storage or retrieval system without written consent from the publisher.

All correspondence concerning this book should be addressed to Track of the Wolf Inc.

ISBN 0-9765797-0-7

Credits

Photography: Ryan R. Gale, David S. Ripplinger, Ethan R. Ripplinger

Designer: Ryan R. Gale

Contents

Introduction iv	Scrimshaw Your Horn 35
Preface v	Antiquing Techniques 41
Tools & Materials 1	Adding Patina. 43
How to Choose a Horn. 4	Attaching a Staple 46
Setup Your Workstation 6	Making a Stopper. 48
Cutting & Drilling the Tip 7	The Finished Horn 49
Shaping the Butt. 10	Original Powder Horns 51
Making the Butt Plug. 13	Reproduction Powder Horns . . . 69
Making a Lobed Base 17	Scrimshaw Designs 89
Making a Turned Butt Plug . . . 18	References 91
Shaping the Neck. 21	
Final Finishing the Butt Plug. . . 30	
Staining the Neck. 31	
Securing the Butt Plug 33	

Introduction

Over the last four centuries there have been tens of thousands of gun powder containers made from bone and horn. Both materials more or less impervious to destruction, except from fire and certain types of beetles. I think God was looking ahead, and knew that some day we would need something we could use to keep our powder dry.

The horns quickly became the ideal surface to mark with the identity of the frontiersmen and soldiers. Often illiterate, these men frequently turned to others to decorate their horns for them. You can see how difficult and frustrating it was for them to make their letters, often upside down or backwards, or simply figures that look like letters but didn't spell anything. Generally the figures and drawings on their horns were taken from their immediate surroundings.

By the time of the French and Indian War, the golden period of engraved horns, there were so many skilled and educated craftsmen who were capable of creating powder horns, that they elevated the craft to an art form that is not only beautiful, but shows the personality and the soul of the engraver.

At one time it was thought to be a lost art form, but after seeing what some of our contemporary horn makers like Scott and Cathy Sibley are capable of producing I know I was totally wrong.

Powder horn art is very much alive and well today.

Jim Dresslar
Author
The Engraved Powder Horn

Preface

I have been interested in the history of our country since I was a young boy. I made my first powder horn at the age of ten to go with a flintlock rifle I had cut out of a long plank of wood and whittled to shape with my jack knife.

In 1970 I joined the military. While in the service it was made apparent to me by several officers that I had more of a heritage in this country than I knew about. My stint in the service was cut short when I was injured, and upon my discharge I returned home to enroll in college. During my college tenure I kept delving into my family's genealogy. I discovered that I was tenth generation in this county. I was amazed to find several of my ancestors fought in the French & Indian War and likewise in the Revolutionary War. One of my great, great, great grandfathers, Elnathan Perry, took his father's place in our country's struggle for independence when he was only thirteen years old. Family history has it that he was in three bayonet charges in one day and was grazed on the cheek by a British musket ball. The night before the battle of Yorktown, he was given a shilling to hold Lafayette's horse while he surveyed the site of the up and coming battle. Elnathan's grandson was later shot through both legs on Little Round Top at the battle of Gettysburg, during the American Civil War. All of these tales, along with the coming bicentennial of our country sparked my interest in building muzzle loading rifles and the powder horns that went with them.

As one might expect, my first horns were crude, as was the engraving, which I did myself. My wife Cathy, who is a natural born artist, and is good at anything she tries, wanted to try engraving one of my horns. With her first one done, I was out of a job, and she had inherited one. With that first horn we formed a partnership that endures to this day. We began attending gun shows and rendezvous and were successful in finding new homes for our creations. One thing led to another, and we were soon visiting museums and receiving invitations to visit private collections. It became apparent to us that we needed to stop "creating" horns and start "re-creating" horns. We carefully strive to get the architecture of the horn right, and the style of the engraving correct.

I completed college with a degree in elementary education, and took an offer for a job teaching in an Eskimo village in remote Alaska. This proved to be quite an adventure. It was like stepping back in time! In the mid 1970s, living five hundred miles from the nearest road, store, or hospital, was an experience unlike anything we had ever encountered. Before leaving Anchorage, Cathy would have to place an order for enough food to sustain us for the next nine months! Our supplies arrived by barge from Seattle, and we would have to backpack it to our humble home, a semi-truck trailer!

During the years I taught school at the Alaskan village I filled my spare time re-creating powder horns, using a stump with a nail in it as a work table for lack of anything better. Cathy engraved them and we sold them to our friends back in "civilization", or through ads in magazines like *Muzzle Blasts* or *Muzzleloader*. We kept busy, and always looked forward to corresponding with potential customers and building horns for them. Life in the village was rough, and one had to be self reliant. It gave me a sense of what my ancestors endured playing their part in the building of this nation. As time went on I learned more family history and became more dedicated to my craft. The little "tidbits" of family history drove me to learn more.

This book is a journey of 28 years in the powder horn making business. We are solely self taught. The methods outlined here are those that work for us and will enable the reader to make and engrave their own powder horn with a bare minimum of tools and work space. We have written this book to share our knowledge with those as interested in making powder horns as we are. May the horn you build always keep your powder dry.

Scott Sibley

Tools and Materials List.

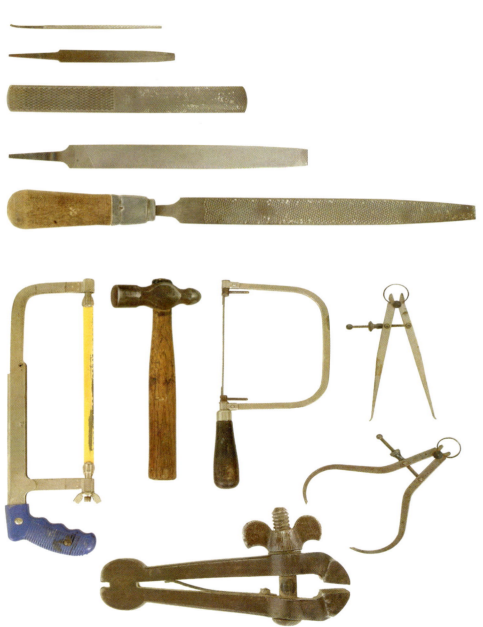

From top to bottom:

- Coarse rat tail file, 4", used for detail work.

- Mill bastard file, 4", used for detail work.

- Rasp, 4 in 1, used for shaping the neck.

- Mill bastard file, 8", used for rough shaping.

- Pattern maker's rasp, used for rough shaping.

- Common hack saw, used for cutting the tip.

- Medium size ball-peen hammer, for setting the plug and nails.

- Coping saw with 5" neck, for cutting out the plug.

- Inside caliper, for measuring the inside of the base.

- Outside caliper, for measuring the outside of the base.

- Hand vise, for putting hand shaped heads on the steel nails used to affix the base plug, if desired.

- Furniture scraper, for scrape finishing the horn.

- Flat sanding block, for flattening the base of the horn after sizing and shaping it perfectly round with a "sizer." Use a coarse belt sander belt. The sanding block is made of a 4" by 11-1/2" piece of plywood. The belt is then slipped over the sanding block. If the fit is a little loose, insert a small wedge in between the block and the belt on either end.

Tools & Preparations

- Small rubber back sanding block. I use 60 grit sand paper to "true" up the surface of the horn, before shaping the tip.

- Duct tape. I use duct tape for layout work. You can also lay out the recessed areas and rings with a pencil or grease pen. I find duct tape works best. It will provide you with a straight edge to follow while making your initial cuts.

- Rit® dyes or similar generic brand, for staining the body and neck:
  2 boxes dark brown
  1 box black
  2 boxes golden yellow
  1 box tangerine

- 'V' gouge and 'U' gouge, used for carving the engrailment around the base of the neck.

- Utility knife. The common utility knife is very useful. It is sharp, and the blade is thin for easy cleanup work. When it gets dull, insert a new blade. Use it in conjunction with the furniture scraper for final finishing of the body.

- Straight wood chisel. I use this for splitting straight grain hard wood, for making the wooden pegs that retain the butt plug.

- Wooden mallet or chaser, used with the gouges to engrail the neck area. I have found from past painful experiences that when cutting horn, it is better and safer to use a chaser. Horn is tough, and requires a lot of force to cut it. One slip, and you will cut yourself deeply.

These tools may be purchased from woodworking, hardware, and craft stores, mail order catalogs, or online.

Recreating the 18th Century Powder Horn

- Wooden sizing plugs are used to form the round butt end of the cow horn, which is normally irregular in shape. Either short or long sizers will do the job.

I use a wood lathe to make my own horn sizers, usually with an 80 degree taper. They can be made of any hardwood or softwood. If you don't have a lathe to turn one, then you will have to shape it by hand. A belt or disc sander works great, just try to get them as round as possible. The large sizer measures 6" tall, 4" in diameter at the base, and 2" in diameter at the tip, with an 80 degree taper. The two smaller sizers are made from 2 x 4" lumber. One sizer has a 2-1/2" diameter base and 2" diameter tip, the other has a 3" diameter base, and a 2-1/2" diameter tip. The double sizer can be used for both large and small horns.

How to choose a horn.

Selecting a suitable horn is a personal choice. The perfect horn is in the eye of the beholder. A careful study of original horns will bear this out. These pictures illustrate what I think are very nice horns. The major areas to consider are:

- Curve and twist.
- Base diameter.
- Length.
- Color.

An original powder horn with a very attractive double twist. *Author's collection.*

Raw and Polished Cow Horns.

Recreating the 18th Century Powder Horn

A side view of the cow horn selected for this project.

The cow horn chosen for this project measures 17" around the outer curve, with an attractive twist. The body is mostly white, with some light brown areas, and a dark brown tip. This horn was purchased already cleaned and polished, which saves you the time and trouble of having to do it yourself. As you can see, the butt is far from round. Most horns have an irregular shaped butt end, which can easily be shaped round using the steps and techniques outlined in this book.

Tools & Preparations

Setup Your Workstation.

For this project I selected a sturdy metal table with a large, securely mounted vise. A round piece of wood is clamped in the vise jaws, which is used to support the horn while working. A heavy piece of leather with a hole cut in the center fits over the round wooden peg to protect the horn from the hard edges of the vise. Along with sufficient light, this small setup provides ample workspace and a stable platform.

To successfully make a powder horn, you must have a sturdy rest to support your work. A fancy setup is not necessary. When Cathy and I resided in the Alaskan bush, a tree stump with a large nail hammered into it was our setup for making powder horns. Your setup needs to be sturdy, not complicated.

Cutting & Drilling the Tip.

1. Measure the inner cavity depth.

2. Mark the cavity depth.

An inside view of a raw cow horn showing the depth of the inner cavity. Notice the long solid tip, and how the thickness of the walls increase towards the tip.

Figure 1. Measure the depth of the inner cavity with a piece of heavy wire. An old coat hanger works great! The wire needs to be straight and flexible enough to follow the curve of the horn. Insert the wire into the horn's inner cavity. Press it up against the outside curvature of the horn. Mark or hold the wire where it comes even with the outer edge of the opening or "base" of the horn.

Figure 2. Remove the wire from the inner cavity, and place it along the outer curve. Mark the end of the inside cavity on the outside of the horn with a pencil or soft tip marker. This will indicate how much solid tip needs to be drilled to connect the hollow cavity.

Figure 3. After marking the end of the horn's inner cavity, you need to mark a second line where the tip of the horn should be cut off. The space between the two lines should be as straight as possible to aid in drilling a straight hole. The distance between the lines should be no longer than the length of your drill bit.

Cutting & Drilling the Tip

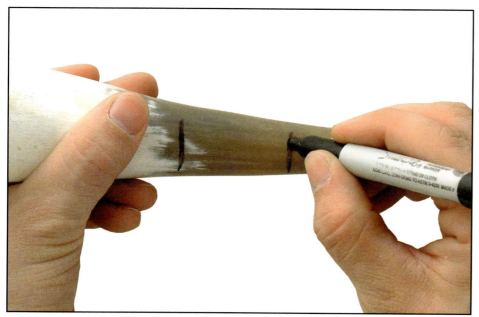

3. Mark the tip where it will be cut off.

4. Cut the tip.

5. Mark the center of the tip.

You want to leave as much of the tip as possible for aesthetics, but too much tip can lead to trouble, such as drilling through the side of the horn, I have done it many times.

Figure 4. Having determined how much of the tip you can drill through, cut the tip off along your mark with a hack saw or coping saw. Place the horn on the leather covered vise, pressing the horn firmly against the wooden peg for support when cutting.

Figure 5. Mark the center of the cut tip with an 'X', to aid in positioning the center point for drilling your pouring hole. Next, draw a straight reference line from the cut end of the horn, to the line marking the location of the inner cavity. Use a ruler along this line to determine the depth of the hole you need to drill.

6. Select a drill bit.

7. Drill the pouring hole.

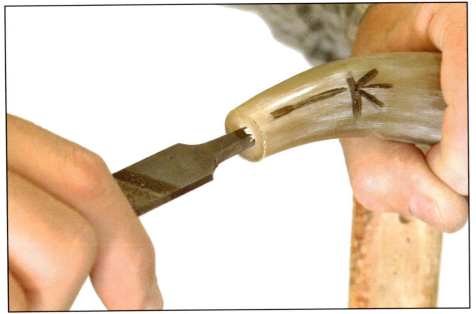

8. Taper the pouring hole.

Figure 6-7. Select a drill bit 1/4" to 1/2" in diameter. Original powder horns have a variety of pouring holes sizes. This could be the original maker's personal taste, or simply the size of drill bit he had on hand. Hold the horn securely in your hand and rest it against your support. Your reference line must be visible to use as your guide. Center your drill bit on the "X" that you drew. Slowly drill your hole until you drill through the solid tip, and into the hollow inner cavity.

Figure 8. Taper the pouring hole with a rat-tail file, or as I do, by grinding sharp edges on the tang of a 10" file. Both of these methods serves the purpose adequately. If using the sharpened file tang, don't be too aggressive, as it may split the tip. When tapering is complete, I suggest putting a little powder in the horn to see how it flows. If the powder does not flow smoothly, check for burrs, and remove them with your rat tail file. If the pouring hole needs to be enlarged, enlarge the hole by only one drill bit size at a time. Remember, it is always easier to enlarge an opening, but difficult to make it smaller.

Shaping the Butt

Figure 9. Shaping the butt requires softening the horn's base to make it flexible enough to press onto a rounding or sizing cone, which will hereafter be referred to as a "sizer". I use three different methods, depending on the horn.

- Hot vegetable or peanut oil method.
- Boiling water method.
- Paint stripper or heat gun.

For safety reasons, you will need eye protection, leather gloves, and a work apron. I recommend doing this outside, not on your stove.

Vegetable cooking oil or peanut oil can get very hot. If you are not watching carefully you can burn your horn. You will need a large coffee can or old cooking pot. Add cooking oil to a depth of two to three inches. Use a candy thermometer to monitor the temperature. When the oil reaches the 350 to 375 degree range, shut off your heat source. This will reduce the fire danger. Wearing eye protection and gloves, put the base of the horn into the hot oil. Remove the horn from the oil after five or six seconds, and check to see if it has softened enough by pinching it with a gloved hand as in **Figure 11**. If it is pliable enough, press it on the sizing cone and allow it to cool as shown in **Figure 12**. If it is still not pliable enough, place it back in the hot oil for another five or six seconds and test again. After cooling, you will need to wash the horn with soap and water to remove the oil residue.

I use the hot oil technique for very stubborn horns and horns with lathe turned butt plugs. Horns that have been softened with hot oil will retain their round shape better than with any other method, which makes fitting the plug much easier. But, if you are not careful, you can ruin your horn by leaving it in the oil too long.

The boiling water method is a clean and easy way to heat the base, but is more time consuming. Simply dip the horn base in a pot of boiling water. Check it every few minutes with a gloved hand until it is pliable enough to place on your sizing cone. There is a lot less chance of burning your horn using boiling water, but the horn does not keep its shape as well as with the other methods.

9. Soften the butt in hot water or oil.

10. Soften the butt with hot air.

11. Check for flexibility.

12. Place the horn on the sizer.

Figure 10. A paint stripper or heat gun is a quick and effective method of softening the horn base. Because of it's high temperature and dry heat, you can ruin a horn if the heat gun is held in one spot for too long. A heat gun is less dangerous than using hot oil. Apply the heat around the base of the horn, and check frequently for flexibility.

Figure 11. When using any of the three methods to heat the base of the horn, check frequently for flexibility, and be sure to wear gloves to keep from burning your hands.

Figure 12. When the horn is flexible, place it firmly on the horn sizer as shown and allow to cool. Remove the horn from the sizing cone when cool. If you used the hot oil method, now is the time to wash the inside and outside of the horn with dish detergent to remove the oil film. If you need to delay working on your horn at this point, leave the horn on the sizer until you can resume work.

Shaping the Butt

13. Mark the base of the horn.

14. Trim the base of the horn.

Figure 13. Scrutinize the angle of the powder horn base. The base determines the overall look of the horn, and is very important to the finished appearance. The base of the horn will probably be ragged and uneven and needs to be trimmed. Use a strip of duct tape to mark an even edge, this determines the amount to be trimmed off.

Figure 14. Use a mill bastard file to remove the excess horn above your duct tape guide. Notice how the horn is braced against the vise mounted post for stability. Having the luxury of a belt or disk sander will make this process a lot easier than doing it by hand.

Figure 15. Sand the base perfectly flat. I use a flat block of wood, 4" by 11-1/2", and slide a medium grit sander belt over it. Check the flatness of your horn by placing it on a truly flat surface.

15. Flatten the base of the horn.

Making the Butt Plug.

16. Trace the butt onto your wood.

17. Clamp the wood in your vice.

Measuring the plug diameter with an inside caliper.

Figure 16. Historically, most powder horns had flat to slightly domed plugs of soft wood. Soft wood is light weight and easily worked, which makes it the best choice. Use 1/2" thick white pine for flat plugs, and 3/4" thick for slightly domed plugs. Examine your powder horn and select the butt plug style you like. I have decided that this horn should have a slightly domed plug.

Place the butt of your horn on the plug material and trace around it. You can use inside calipers or outside calipers and finally use a compass to draw a round circle on the wood, but that is not necessary. This is not a terribly complicated procedure.

Figure 17-18. If you selected a domed plug, then make the diameter of the plug about 1/8" larger than the tracing of the horn butt. Cut out the plug using a coping saw, sabre saw, or band saw. The more accurate the cut, the less fine fitting has to be done. Your clean up can be done with a file, sanding block, belt sander, or disc sander. The latter two speed things up considerably. Of course, traditionalists will stick with traditional tools.

Making the Butt Plug

18. Cut the domed butt plug slightly oversized.

19. File a tapered edge on the plug.

Figure 19. Rasp or sand the edge of the plug flush with your drawn line. Next, file a taper on the plug so it fits snugly in the base of the horn. The taper of the plug should be approximately 80 degrees. Again, an electric sander will save you a lot of time here. Plugs only need to fit on the outside rim of the horn's base. A horn's inner cavity is irregular to say the least. To spend a lot of time fitting the plug to the inner cavity is not necessary.

Figure 20. Place the rough butt plug into the base of the horn. Note how much protrudes from the horn as shown in the photo.

Fitting a turned butt plug is considerably more difficult. Your measurements must be precise, and the base of the horn's inner cavity must be perfectly round, otherwise it will look sloppy. This is an advanced procedure which will be covered in depth on page 18.

20. Test the fit of the rough base plug.

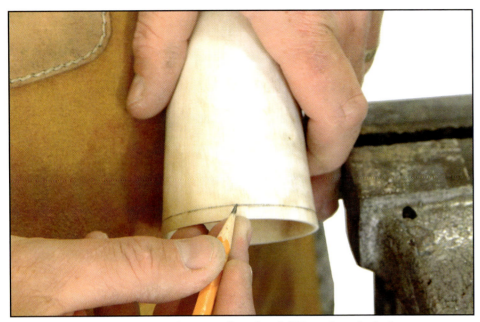

21. Draw a reference line for drilling the pin holes.

22. Draw reference lines on the plug for the pin holes.

23. Tap the base plug to seat it.

Figure 21. Remove the butt plug. Draw a line around the base of your horn, about a 1/4" above the base, as a reference for drilling the holes for your pins. Use a drawing compass, or simply use your finger and a pencil to mark your line.

Figure 22. Lay out the lines for the nails or pegs on your butt plug. The number of nails or pegs is your choice. Divide up the base with equal distance between the pegs. Most original horn makers kept the number of pegs to a minimum. I recommend using at least five pegs, evenly spaced.

Figure 23. Resting the horn on a bag of shot, or sand bag, tap the plug in place with a small hammer. Don't hit it too hard, or you risk cracking the base. Using the marks you made on the plug as a guide, draw matching marks around the base of your horn where the pin holes will be drilled.

Making the Butt Plug

Figure 24. Remove the butt plug. Use an electric or hand drill to drill the pilot holes on your intersecting lines for some temporary nails. These same holes will be used later to install permanent pegs. The photo shows a 5/64" drill bit in an electric hand drill for use with 18 gauge nails. Select a drill bit the same size as the nails you are using. Once done, be sure to file off any burrs that the drill may have raised inside the horn.

If your base plug fits well, put a thin layer of wood glue on the plug and tap it into place. Blow through the horn to make sure it is air tight. If not, tap the plug a few more times, and re-check it for an air tight seal. If your plug doesn't fit the horn opening precisely, don't fret! Soften the horn by heating it in boiling water, or using a heat gun. For seating the plug, boiling water is the best, as it softens the inside of the horn, forming a gummy, natural glue. I still use a small amount of wood glue on the butt plug. Tap the plug in place and blow through the horn checking for leaks.

Figure 25. Tap in some temporary nails. I use 5/8" 18 gauge nails to hold the plug in place while the glue dries. Leave the nails part way out so you can easily remove them before final finishing the outside surface of the horn. Allow enough time for the glue to harden and the horn to cool.

Plugs were generally secured with iron nails, brass tacks, or wooden pegs. I will demonstrate how to make your own wooden pegs later. If you choose to use wooden pegs, then you may remove the temporary nails and fit the wooden pegs to the base at this time. DO NOT put the final metal nails, pins or tacks in yet. They will interfere with scraping the body.

24. Drill pilot holes for temporary nails.

25. Seat the plug, and tap in some temporary nails.

Making a Lobed Base.

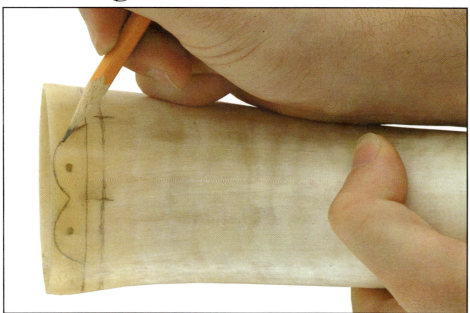

26. Draw the lobe with a pencil.

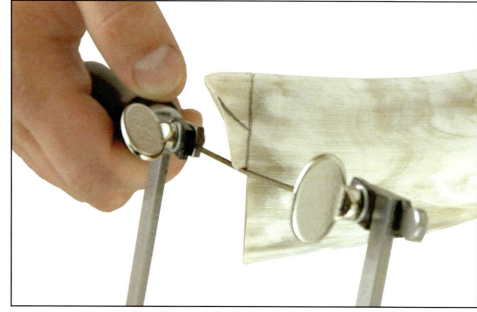

27. Cut out the base around the lobe.

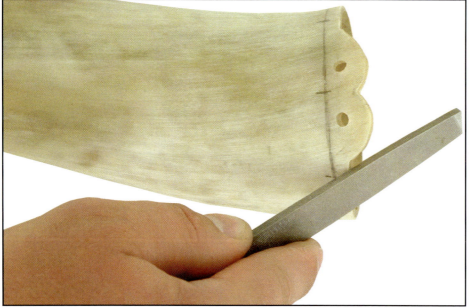

28. File the lobe and base smooth, and drill the holes.

Figure 26. An extension of the horn base or "lobe" was popular during the 1750's. A single or double lobe was cut into the horn which extended beyond the plug. Two holes were then drilled for fastening a strap. These lobes were sometimes highly carved or scrimshawed. To make a double lobe, first draw the design into the horn with a sharp pencil. A ring should then be drawn at the base of the lobe around the horn. This will be the base of your powder horn.

Figure 27. Cut out the lobe with a coping saw, being careful to follow the layout line for the base of the horn.

Figure 28. File the lobe and base smooth with a mill bastard file. Drill the holes used for tying the strap. A 3/16" drill bit works great. You can now install the butt plug. Most horns of this style had flat butt plugs, though some were domed.

Making a Turned Butt Plug.

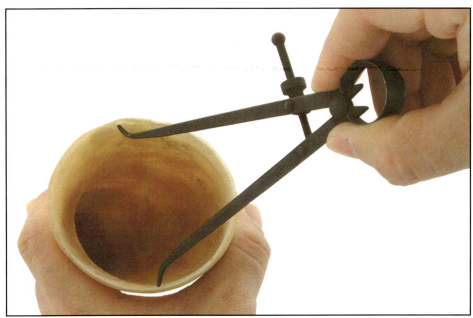

29. Measure the inside base diameter.

30. Mount a suitable piece of round wood on the lathe.

Figure 29-30. Turning a butt plug really complicates the horn making process, and requires more than a little skill, but it adds appeal to the finished horn. You must be proficient with a lathe, so before you tackle your first lathe turned plug, please spend some time learning how to use it safely, and learn how to sharpen the tools. To make a turned butt plug, the base of your horn needs to be as round as possible, and perfectly flat for the best appearance. Measure the inside diameter of the horn base, and figure out how large the butt plug must be, then choose a piece of wood of suitable diameter.

Figure 31. Turn a hollow in the butt plug. Many original horns had hollowed out plugs to hold more powder, and some did not. Mine always do. Hollow out the end and cut the recessed shoulder that fits into the horn. Remember, precise measurements are required. When cutting the shoulder, keep track of your progress with your calipers. When you get it close, take it off your lathe and try it on your horn.

31. Turn the hollow cavity and shoulder.

32. Turn the base over on your lathe, and shape the outside.

33. Turn a decorative knob in the base.

34. Sand the plug smooth.

If it fits the first time, you are either very good or lucky, if not, continue to trim the shoulder. Put pencil marks on the tapered area and twist it inside the horn. This will show you where more has to be taken off. When you get a desirable fit, check to see if the base of the horn is truly flat, and that it is flush against the base all the way around.

Figure 32. Turn the plug over on your lathe (if you have a chuck that allows you to). Shape the outside as you wish. A reference book is a good source for ideas. A decorative knob is often turned into the plug for attaching a horn strap. Inlays or staples can be inset into the base of the butt plug as well.

Figure 33. The rough plug with a decorative knob for a horn strap.

Figure 34. With the plug spinning in the lathe, use a sanding block and sand paper to sand the surface smooth.

Making a Turned Butt Plug

35. Add reference lines for cutting rings.

36. Cut the rings with a gouge.

Figure 35. Decorative rings are often cut into turned plugs. This will be a "beehive" style butt plug. A quick way to draw evenly spaced lines is to use a pencil and ruler while the plug is spinning on the lathe.

Figure 36. Turn the rings with an appropriate gouge on your layout lines.

Figure 37. Sand smooth any burrs or rough edges on the plug. When your turned plug is finished, attach it to your horn using pins or nails.

37. Remove the plug from the lathe and install.

Shaping the Neck.

38. Layout the neck and shoulders.

39. Make a shallow cut to indicate the ring.

40. Make a shallow cut around the shoulder.

Figure 38. To begin shaping the neck, use a pencil or felt tip pen to mark the shoulder and rings. When you like the proportions, use thin strips of duct tape to mark where you will begin your cuts. A good reference book will give you ideas, and help you keep your designs traditional. Use the collection of original and reproduction horns in the back of this book for inspiration, or try making your own designs.

Figure 39-40. With a standard hack saw, lightly cut along the edge of the tape. This makes it much easier to keep your shoulders straight and clean. A mill bastard file will also work.

Figures 41-42. After cutting the delineating marks with the hack saw, use the mill bastard file to remove the horn away from your mark. Do not file this area to final depth. You must leave enough horn to file flats or other decorative carving. If your neck is going to be round, you can file it to its final depth now.

Shaping the Neck

41. Lightly file back the edges around the ring and shoulder.

42. The neck after cutting and filing.

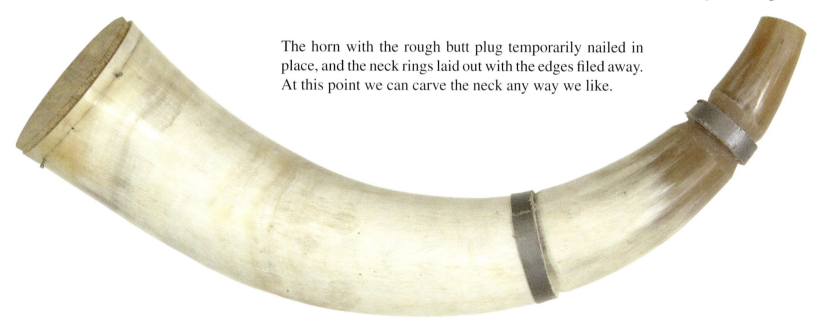

The horn with the rough butt plug temporarily nailed in place, and the neck rings laid out with the edges filed away. At this point we can carve the neck any way we like.

Recreating the 18th Century Powder Horn

43. Divide the neck into quarters, then eighths.

44. Carefully flatten each panel with a rasp.

Figure 43. Octagonal neck flats were very popular, and found on many original horns. I decided to carve the neck of this horn with eight flats. Begin by laying out four equally spaced lines around the horn with a felt tip marker. Divide each of those flats in half, to get eight equal flats.

Figure 44-45. Shape the flats with your 4 in 1 rasp or the pattern maker's rasp. Be sure to work away from the shoulder. A careful eye and cautious cutting is needed. On the concave section of the horn, use the half round face of the file, and on the convex surface of the horn, use the flat surface of the file. Continue the same process on the horn tip. Keep your panels even and flowing with the overall appearance of the neck.

45. The flats should flow smoothly through the neck.

Shaping the Neck

46. Use a mill bastard file when working near the edges.

47. Make sure your panels are proportional to each other.

Figure 46-47. When working close to the shoulders, use the mill bastard file, it is less aggressive than the 4 in 1 rasp, and less likely to remove too much horn. The raised shoulders of the ring and body need to be as clean and crisp as possible for the best appearance.

Roll the horn in your hand, and carefully check to see if your panels are proportional to each other. The panels need to flow with the overall shape of the horn. The concave and convex surfaces should flow with the natural curve of the neck, rather than in contrast. If not, file them until they flow correctly. This subtle shaping is what makes a modern horn maker's work stand out, and look more historically accurate.

Figure 48. When you are satisfied with your lines, clean up the rough surfaces with the mill bastard file. Pay careful attention to the shoulders of the ring and body, keeping them square and clean.

48. Smooth the rough surfaces, and square the edges.

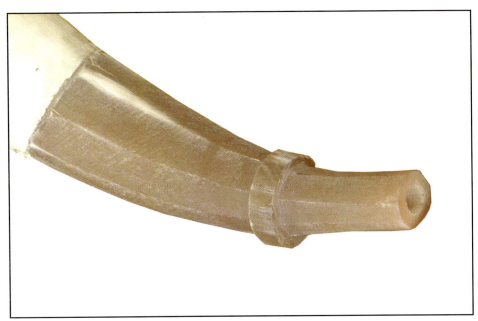

49. The neck is shown with rough finished flats.

50. Draw a line along the center of the ring.

Figure 49. The neck is shown with the finished rough flats. The flats still need to be finished smooth, but first I want to add more detail to the neck and head.

Figure 50-51. I decided to split the ring that holds the horn strap into two. Using a pencil, draw a line along the center. Use a 4" rat tail file to carefully file a parting line. Continue until the groove is pleasing to your eye. Be careful about the depth, as you don't want to file through the horn.

Study original horns for alternative ways to carve the neck rings. There are countless other ways it can be done. Some horns have very fancy rings while others have plain ones. Some horns use iron staples instead of rings to attach a shoulder strap.

51. Use a rat tail file to split the ring in two.

Shaping the Neck

52. Draw a spout ring near the mouth.

53. File a groove away from your pencil mark.

Figure 52-53. Spout tips often have a raised ring or "Head". If you want to add a raised ring on the tip of the spout, now is the time to put one there. This is purely a personal choice. Many old horns had rings, many did not. Begin by drawing a line around the tip, use a ruler if you need to help keep it even. Using the 4" rat tail file, put a groove around the head. Don't go too deep, just enough to give some depth and detail to the tip.

Figure 54. Using the mill bastard file, relieve the neck of the horn a small amount, leaving a raised ring. It doesn't take much depth to show the detail, if you keep the edges smooth and clean. Notice how I use the post as a support and stop, so I don't touch the raised ring with the file. Work carefully, pay attention to detail, and do not be too aggressive.

Figure 55. Round the corners of the ring with a fine file, both on the inside and outside as shown on the next page. Finally, clean up the shaping wherever necessary with a fine file, or by scraping with a sharp knife.

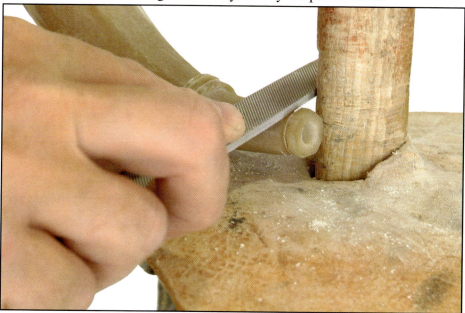

54. Flatten the panels to reveal the raised head.

55. File the corners of the ring round.

56. Start the engrailment at the bottom of the horn.

Figure 56-58. Carving engrailing around the neck adds a beautiful touch to a horn. Many horns have no engrailment. Study the horns in the later portion of this book to help select a pattern. I selected an alternating 'V' and 'U' gouge design. Lay out a perimeter line with a pencil just behind the neck. You will need an assistant to hold the horn, a shot or sand bag to cushion the horn, a chaser, and wood gouges of the appropriate size and shape. Cutting horn is much like wood, only more brittle, so work with light blows. Hold the chisel, as shown in **Figure 57**, and slowly lower the angle of the cut to lift the chip out as shown in **Figure 58**. Don't carve the designs deeper than the surface of the neck, or you will have to touch up the flats again. It may be a wise idea to divide the area you are going to carve into sections with a pencil. Start at the bottom and work your way around. If the last two cuts don't line up, the error will be less visible at the bottom of the horn.

Figure 59. Using a mill bastard file or sharp knife, go back and clean the flats you may have cut with the gouge while cutting the engrailment.

57. Begin each cut at a right angle to the horn.

Shaping the Neck

58. Lower the chisel while hammering to lift the chip.

59. Touch up any cut marks you made while carving the engrailment.

With the carving complete, we will clean the neck and head of any file marks, and scrape it perfectly smooth.

60. Scrape each flat smooth with a sharp knife.

61. Light scraping will produce a polished surface.

Figure 60-61. Scrape the flat neck areas to remove any file marks. Use a sharp utility knife. Pull the knife slowly toward you. Be careful not to cut yourself! Once you get a feel for using a scraper, you will never go back to sandpaper. Lighten up on the pressure, and you can produce an almost polished surface. Using the edge of the sharp utility knife, carefully cut along the rings to make the inside corners perfectly square. After scraping the neck to your desired finish, use smooth steel wool to achieve a finer finish.

Figure 62. Remove any file marks left by the file in shaping the rings and other curved surfaces of the horn tip. A sponge sanding block works very well for this step, because it forms to the curves. A rubber backed sanding block will also work well.

62. Clean curved surfaces with a sponge sanding block.

Final Finishing the Butt Plug

63. Shape the butt plug with a rasp.

64. Sand the edges flush with the horn.

Figure 63. Next, shape and finish the butt plug. We could have shaped it earlier, but I prefer to carve the neck while the glue drys. This horn features a slightly domed plug. Using a rasp, file the edge of the wood nearly flush with the base of the horn, and rough out the basic domed shape. If you have an electric belt or disc sander in your shop, by all means use them, they are great labor saving tools. If you prefer a flat plug, then flatten it to your satisfaction.

Figure 64. Using a sanding block, sand the edges flush with the base of the horn and smooth the butt plug to its final shape.

Figure 65. Finish the plug by scraping it with a sharp furniture scraper. Scrape along the grain, and not across it. This is a great way to eliminate sanding marks. Scraping is much easier and faster than sanding with progressively finer grit sand papers.

65. Scrape the plug smooth with a furniture scraper.

Staining the Neck.

66. Bring water to a boil and add dye.

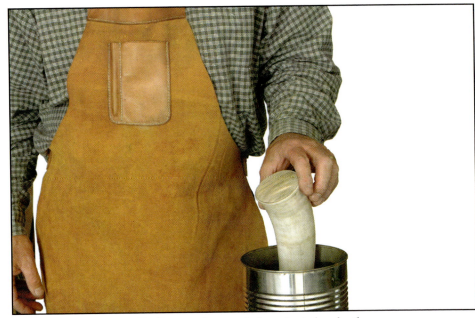

67. Insert the neck into hot dye bath.

68. After 20 to 60 minutes, remove the horn.

Figure 66. The next step will be to dye the neck area. I stain the necks of most of my horns. It greatly enhances the look of the finished horn. Of course, if the horn you choose to make has no recessed neck, then you can't stain it. To stain the neck, I use a coffee can or similar container, two packages of dark brown Rit® or similar dye, and a pinch or two of black dye. Fill your container 3/4 full of water and bring it to a boil. Reduce the heat and stir in the dye. Bring it to a boil again, then shut off the heat.

Figure 67. Place the horn into the hot dye bath for five minutes. Remove the horn, and check the surface area of the neck for finishing marks, they show up very well at this stage. If you find any marks, remove them with careful scraping and steel wool. Place the horn back in the dye bath for another 20 to 60 minutes. When satisfied with the color, remove it from the bath.

Figure 68. Don't worry if the body gets stained along with the neck as shown. There is no way to avoid this. It will be scraped off later.

Staining the Neck

69. Scrape the excess stain to reveal the engrailing.

70. Scrape the excess stain from the body.

Figure 69-70. Remove the excess stain on the body above the neck. I prefer a furniture scraper for this job. You may use a sanding block if you wish, but it takes longer to sand away the stain, and you create more horn dust. When you are scraping towards the neck, use your thumb as a stop so you don't accidentally scrape the dye off the neck. If this happens, you may have to re-stain it.

Figure 71. Scrape the rest of the horn body to remove any scratches and file marks. If you temporarily nailed the base plug in place as shown earlier in the book, now is the time to remove the nails, as they will be in the way while scraping the body of the horn. I scrape the surface of the body three times, or until it is free of blemishes.

71. Scrape the body three times, or until free of blemishes.

Securing the Butt Plug.

72. Split a piece of hard wood into 1/8" thick sheets.

73. Split the wood into 1/8" square pegs..

Next, attach the butt plug permanently. Make your own pegs, nails, or pins to fasten the plug. Traditionally you have four choices:

1. Wooden pegs
2. Nails
3. Metal pins
4. Brass tacks

Figure 72-73. Wooden pegs are quite easily made from straight grain hardwood. A 1/2" to 1" thick scrap piece of wood will make several pegs. Use a straight chisel and hammer to split square pegs from the block of wood. Round wooden toothpicks are a cheap and easy alternative.

Figure 74. Use a sharp utility knife. Roughly carve the peg round and put a point on one end.

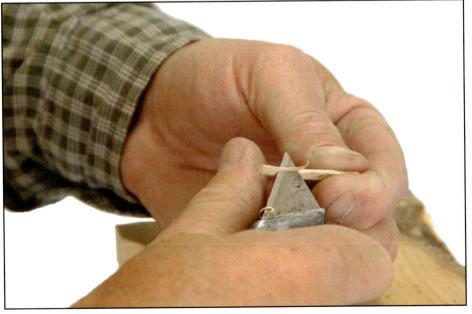

74. Carve the wooden pegs round, and add a point.

Securing the butt plug

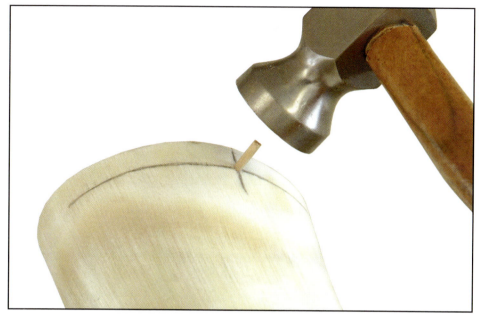

75. Hammer the pegs into place.

76. Trim the pegs flush with the horn.

Figure 75. Use the holes you drilled for the temporary nails for installing your permanent wooden pegs. Enlarge the holes if you want larger pegs. Apply a little wood glue to a peg, and lightly hammer it into place.

Figure 76. With a sharp knife, cut the peg flush with the horn. Do not break the peg off. It will not be as smooth as when cutting it off with a sharp knife. Wipe away any excess glue from the horn.

Figure 77. Nails are most often used to retain butt plugs. Since small handmade nails are largely unavailable, you must make your own. You don't need to hand forge a nail, simply re-shape an existing one! Whichever size you go with, the re-shaping process is the same.

Secure the nail in a hand vise. Use the ball on your small ball-peen hammer, and carefully shape the nail head to resemble an old handmade nail. If you want a plain metal pin for your horn, simply cut the head off of a nail and file it smooth.

77. Reshaping a nail head.

Recreating the 18th Century Powder Horn

Scrimshaw your Horn.

Tools.

These are the basic tools used by Cathy to scrimshaw a powder horn:

- A cloth bag filled with dry beans, serves to cradle the horn.

- Gloves, helps prevent blisters, and protect the hand.

- A sharp pencil and eraser, for drawing the designs.

- Two sharp knifes. The smaller knife is much like an X-acto® knife (shown below), used for fine scrimshaw work. The second larger blade is for thicker scrimshaw.

- A drawing compass, for drawing perfect circles on the horn.

These tools can be found in woodworking catalogs, magazines, hardware and craft stores.

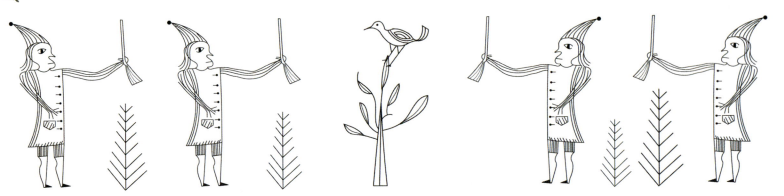

78. Draw two border lines around the butt.

79. Incise the borders around the butt.

80. Evenly divide the space, and pencil in a zig-zag pattern.

The first thing you must do is to select a theme or design for your horn. There are several good reference books that will give you lots of ideas. This particular horn will be a rendition of a horn from Jim Dresslar's book *"The Engraved Powder Horn"*.

Figure 78. Place the horn on the bean filled bag for stability. Draw two parallel lines around the base. Use your fingers as a depth gauge as shown in the photo. A soft sharp pencil is recommended for drawing your designs. A drawing compass can also be used for drawing straight lines and arcs.

Figure 79. Incise the lines around the base of the horn using the X-acto® type knife. The cuts do not need to be overly deep. Cut slowly and carefully so your blade does not slip. Wear a leather glove to protect your hand when cutting.

Figure 80. Pencil in the next design element, a zig-zag pattern between the two lines. A ruler may be used to evenly divide the space.

81. Cut long lines slowly, or as a series of small cuts.

82. Add decorative dots using a knife point.

Figure 81. Cut the next part of the design using the X-acto® knife. Add some diagonal lines inside the triangles. Cut slowly around long lines to keep them straight. Instead of making one long cut, try making several smaller cuts. Crooked lines will be very visible after they are darkened.

Figure 82. Add some decorative dots around the engrailment using the tip of a plain knife. The tip of the knife is rotated like a drill to create small round decorative dots. The tip of a drill bit could also be used.

Figure 83. Lay out two parallel lines around the neck using a sharp pencil. Use a ruler if you need, to help keep your lines even.

83. Draw a border around the neck base.

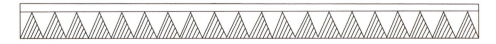

Scrimshaw Your Horn

84. Incise the border around the neck base.

85. Draw or transfer your main design onto the body.

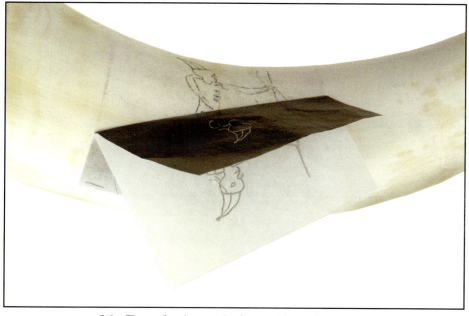

86. Transferring a design with carbon paper.

Figure 84. Incise the parallel lines around the neck using the X-acto® knife. Border designs do not need to be complicated. Most original horns do not even have border work, and those that do are very simple in design. Border art adds that extra touch to the finished horn.

Figure 85. Lay out the central theme or design element on the horn. We use Dresslar's *"The Engraved Powder Horn"* book as a source for ideas much of the time. For this subject I have selected a French and Indian War horn from his book. Draw the designs using a soft lead pencil. Now you are ready to start cutting the design.

Figure 86. If you are not able to draw freehand, use lightweight tracing paper and carbon paper to trace and transfer designs. Place the tracing paper over the design you want to put on the horn, and trace it with a pencil. Tape it on the horn with a piece of carbon paper of the same size behind it. Trace the design through the carbon paper and on to the horn, as shown.

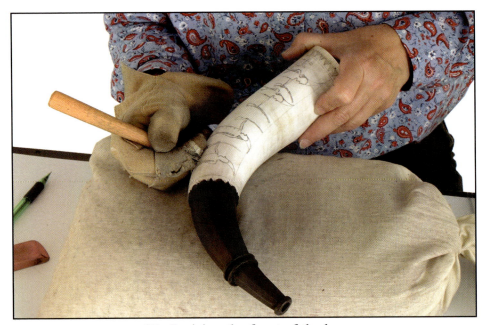

87. Incising the front of the horn.

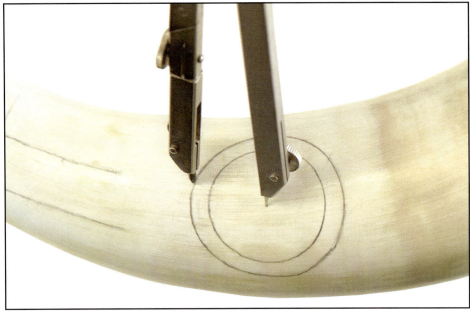

88. Use a drawing compass to draw perfect circles.

Figure 87. The design from Dresslar's book is engraved with the X-acto® knife. Work from one side to the other, and try to avoid smearing your pencil drawings.

Figure 88. Use a drawing compass to draw perfect circles, even on curved surfaces. Be careful when cutting around circles or objects with tight curves, as it is very easy to slip. Take your time and cut slowly. For small designs, try making several small cuts instead of one long cut.

Figure 89-90. Draw and incise the remainder of your horn. After the horn is completely engraved, use fine sand paper to take off the burrs raised during cutting.

HONI · SOIT · QVI · MAL · Y · PENSE

"Honi Soit Qui Mal Y Pense" (shame to him who thinks ill of it). The motto of the Most Noble Order of the Garter, which surrounds the royal arms of Great Britain.

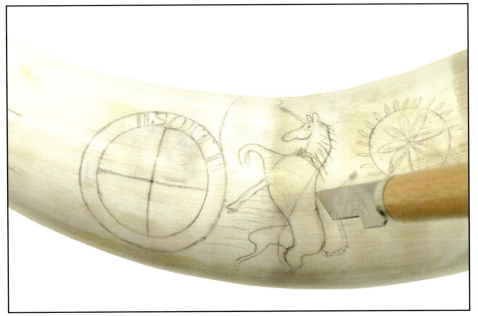

89. Incising the back of the horn.

Scrimshaw Your Horn

The image below shows the design cut in, but there is a lot of detail work left. To darken the incised lines of the scrimshaw engraving, India ink is used. We use India ink only if the horn is to be left in the white. Apply the ink with a cloth, cotton-ball, or your finger, then wipe away the excess with a damp rag. If the ink stains the horn, simply rub it off with fine steel wool. For an antiqued horn, our antiquing process both ages the horn, and gives color to the scrimshaw. If the horn is to be stained with Rit® dye only, I will apply dark walnut stain with a cloth to darken the scrimshaw. These techniques will be covered in depth later in the book.

90. Lightly sand the burrs off of the scrimshaw.

Antiquing Techniques.

91. Place the horn into the hot dye bath.

92. Remove once you have attained a satisfactory color.

Figure 91-92. There are many theories as to why the old engraved horns have a golden yellow color. No one is certain, but the fact is they do. I know of three methods to create this color on the surface of the horn. I have used all three methods with success.

The first method is to apply "Aquafortis", a commercially prepared mixture of dilute nitric acid and iron. Using it is fairly simple. Wearing rubber gloves, apply Aquafortis to the surface of the horn, and heat it with a heat gun until the surface turns golden. Repeat the process until you get a color you like.

The second method is to dye the surface in a dye bath made of onion skins and apple cider vinegar, mixed with water. A handful of yellow onion skins, about the size of a grapefruit, and a few cups of apple cider vinegar is enough to make a full pot of dye. Bring it to a boil, then turn down the heat. Using a dowel stick, sharpened to go into the pouring hole, I put the horn into the dye bath, checking from time to time for the desired color.

The third method is the one I favor most: Use a turkey boiling pot or similar container. Fill it with enough water to cover the body of the horn, and bring it to a boil. Add two boxes of golden yellow Rit® dye. Check your color on a spare horn. If you like the color, then proceed. If not, alter the color to your taste. I often add a pinch of orange dye to the brew.

The procedure for this method is the same as for the second method. Hold the horn in until you obtain the color you want. Dresslar's book is a great reference for a variety of desired colors and tints.

As shown, the base plug is in the horn while dying. This is why I use a minimum of five fasteners. Some may cringe at this, but it is the technique I have developed and prefer. I sometimes paint the base plug before this step. The hot dye bath will cause the paint to lift, giving the plug an antiqued appearance.

Antiquing Techniques

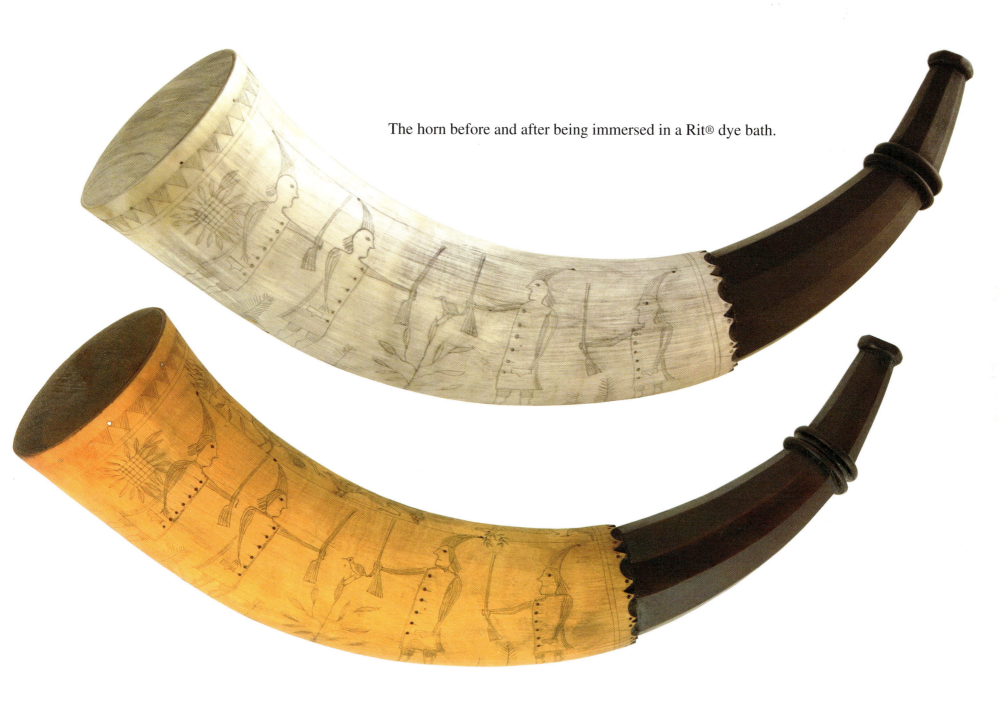

The horn before and after being immersed in a Rit® dye bath.

Adding Patina.

A dyed powder horn ready to be antiqued.

93. Dip the dyed horn into some oil based walnut stain.

Figure 93. Some horn makers like to give their powder horns an aged or dirty look. This "patina" should be applied after the horn is scrimshaw engraved and stained. This process also serves the purpose of darkening the scrimshaw. Dyeing the scrimshaw with India ink is not necessary when applying this finish. The patina finish is also applied to the butt plug and neck to give them an aged look. If you wish to distress your horn, that is, to give it scratches and nicks, that should also be done before this process is started. The patina will build up in these areas giving it a great aged appearance. Distressing should be done liberally. Original horns are a great reference source. Use a utility knife to apply distress marks.

To antique your horn you will need:
- Dark Walnut Stain, oil based (I prefer Star Bronze Co. - Zip Guard® dark walnut stain #30201).
- Black powdered tempera paint.
- Vinyl gloves.
- A cloth.
- A heat gun.

94. As it starts to dry, wipe the stain off with a cloth.

Adding Patina

95. Sprinkle dried tempera paint onto the wet surface.

96. Use a heat gun to dry the horn.

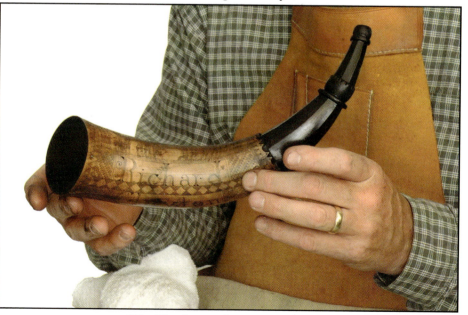

97. The horn after adding patina.

Heat the horn. This helps the patina stick better. It is best to add the patina immediately after staining the horn, while it is still hot. Use a heat gun to re-heat your horn if needed. Fill a container with walnut stain and a little black tempera paint. When the horn is hot, dip the entire horn into the container briefly and remove it.

Figure 94. As the patina dries on the surface, use a cloth dampened with the walnut stain to remove it.

Figure 95. When the horn is still wet, sprinkle dried tempera paint onto the horn. This gives it a nice dirty appearance. You can always remove mistakes with a cloth dampened with stain, that is, until it is dry. Apply the same process to the butt plug and neck.

Figure 96-97. Use your heat gun to help dry the horn, and lock in the finish. Be creative with your antiquing techniques. Try other colors of paint and stains to achieve different effects. Experiment on smaller horns.

Recreating the 18th Century Powder Horn

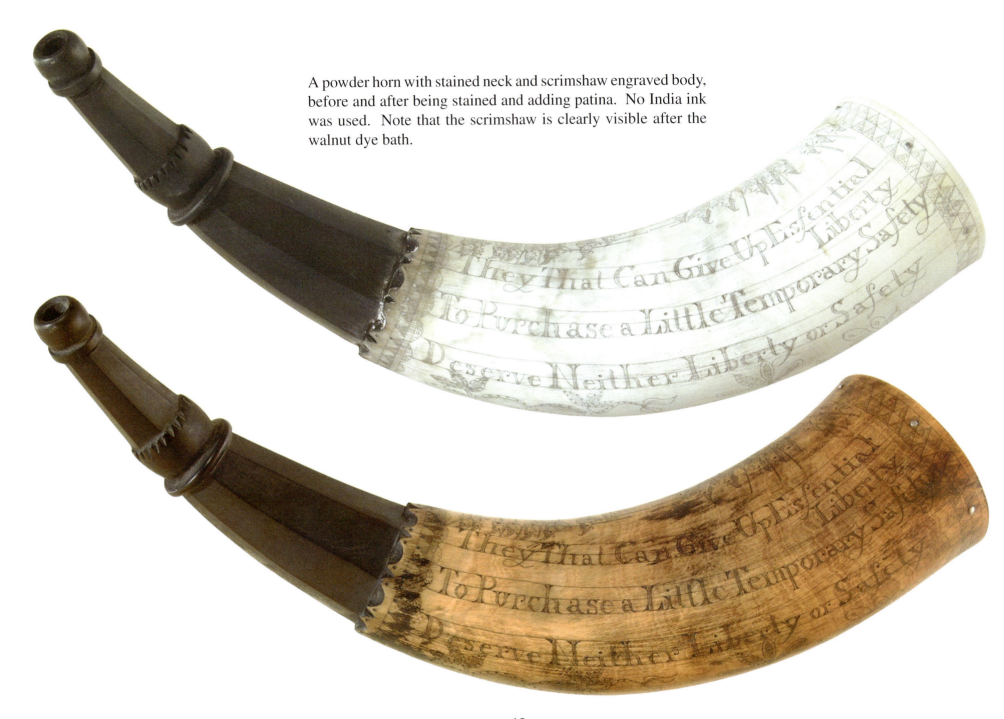

A powder horn with stained neck and scrimshaw engraved body, before and after being stained and adding patina. No India ink was used. Note that the scrimshaw is clearly visible after the walnut dye bath.

Attaching a Staple.

98. Make an iron staple for attaching a shoulder strap.

99. Hammer a piece of wire stock square, or leave round.

Figure 98. Most powder horns were worn over the shoulder using a woven sash or leather strap. There are many methods for attaching a strap. Turned plugs often had a decorative knob turned into the butt. The most common method was to attach an iron or brass staple, nail, screw, or ring. I chose to make an iron staple for this horn. Staples come in a variety of shapes, styles and sizes. Use heavy wire stock, (a wire coat hanger is a great resource).

Figure 99. Start with a four inch long piece of round coat hanger. Hammer it into a square shape, or if you desire, leave it round. Both are correct. Heat the wire with a small torch to make it soft enough to hammer, or hammer it cold. Use gloves and safety glasses when working with torches.

Figure 100. Bend the wire into the shape of a staple. Heat the wire to soften it if needed. Use a pair of pliers to hold the wire in one hand, and another pair to bend it.

100. Heat the wire, and bend it into the shape of a staple.

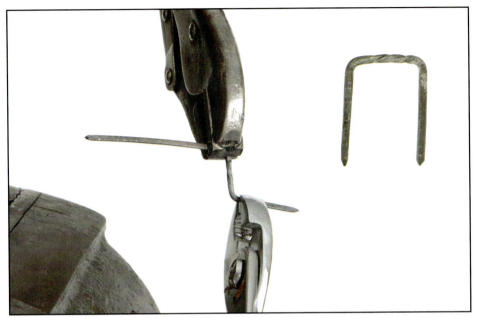

101. Bend a twist into the top of the squared staple.

102. Pre-drill holes into the butt plug.

103. Lightly hammer the staple into place.

Figure 101. Add a decorative twist in the center of your staple. The staple must be made of square stock for the twist to be visible. Lock a Vise-Grip® over the bend to keep it from twisting. Heat the top of the staple with a torch to make it soft enough to twist. Use a pair of pliers to twist the staple 360 degrees. Cut the ends even with a heavy duty wire cutter, and file points on each end. If the staple is crooked, use pliers or a hammer to straighten it.

Figure 102. Using a pencil, mark the butt where the points of the staple are going to be inserted. Pre-drill your holes using an under size drill bit. A little glue may be inserted into the pre-drilled holes for added strength.

Figure 103. Lightly hammer the staple into place. Once the glue dries, your strap can be tied onto the staple. This same process can be used to attach a staple to the neck if desired.

Wooden Stoppers

Making A Stopper

Figure 104. Most original stoppers were very plain. Many were not even tied to the horn. Some horn makers today use fiddle pegs for horn stoppers. I prefer to make my own. I use a soft wood for making my stoppers, typically straight grain white pine. Sometimes the moisture in the air will cause your wooden stopper to expand. An expanding hardwood stopper may break the neck of your horn, while a stopper made of softer wood will give way. I will often stain or antique my stoppers the same way I do the butt plug. Here you can see a variety of common wooden stoppers. The fiddle pegs and turned stoppers can be bought commercially. The right two stoppers I hand carved in a matter of minutes.

Figure 105. I carved this stopper from a 1" x 2" x $5/16$" thick block of wood. Draw the design for your stopper onto the block. Carefully carve away the wood with a sharp carving knife. Remember to always cut away from yourself. The shaft should taper slightly for an air tight seal. This will keep moisture away from the powder. Do not make the shaft longer than necessary, no longer than one inch. Long shafts will often get stuck. When finished, drill a small hole through the head for attaching a thong.

104.

A close-up view of the neck with the carved wooden stopper in place.

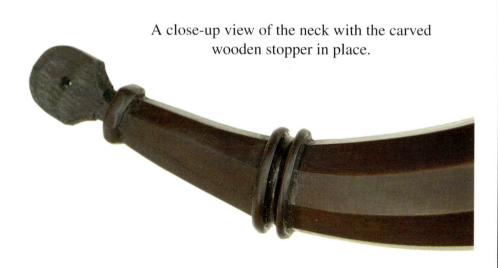

105.

The Finished Horn.

Our featured horn is now completed. The horn has been stained yellow, but has not been antiqued. The horn measures 15" long with a 6" long neck. The domed plug is 3-3/4" diameter with a 1-3/16" staple.

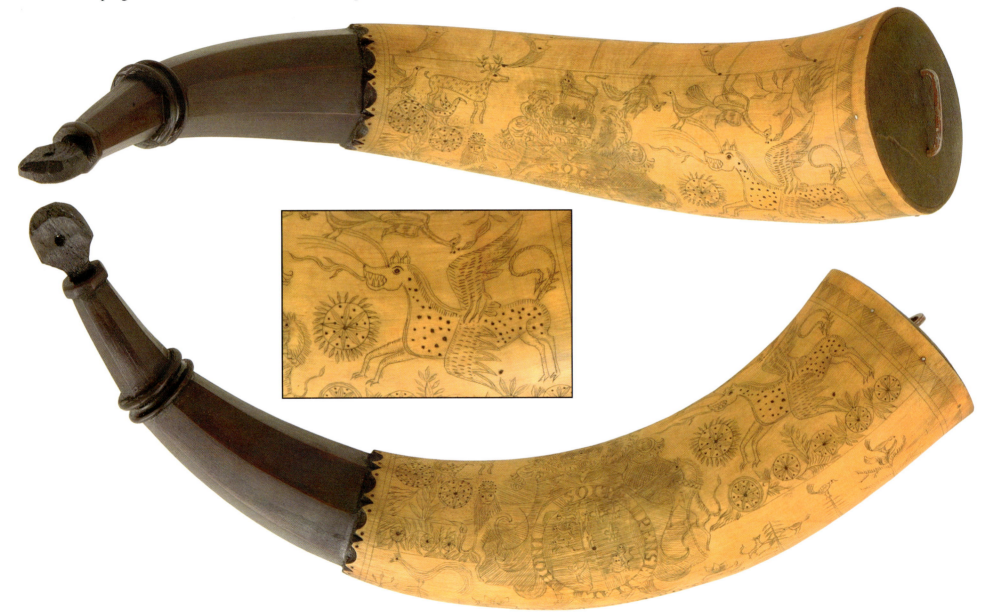

The Finished Horn

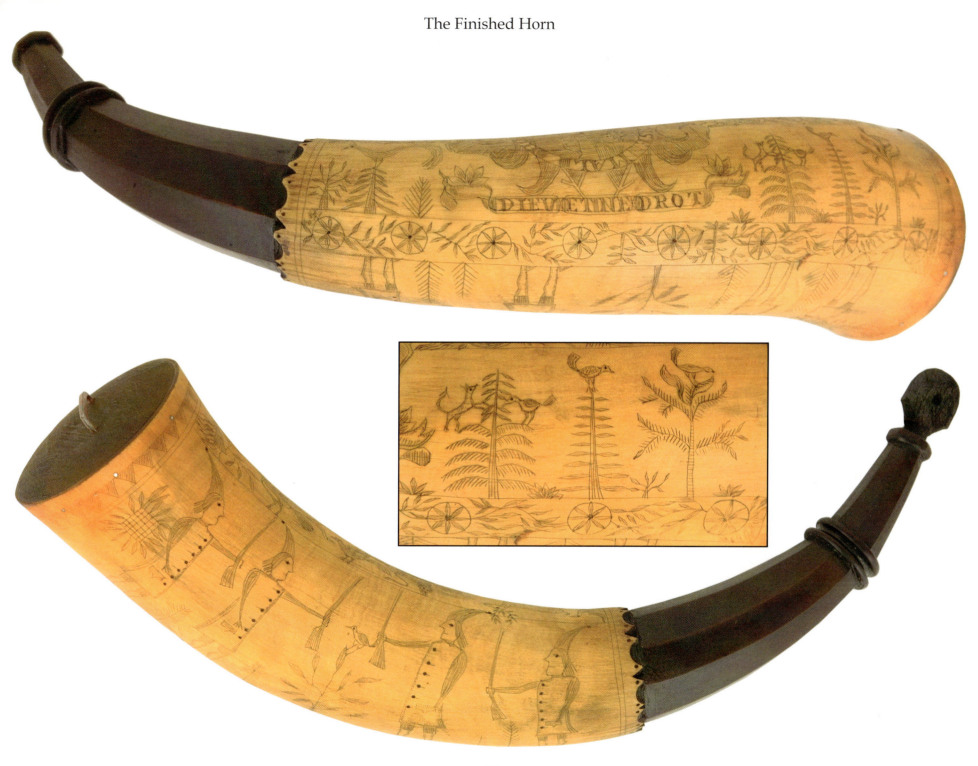

50

Original Powder Horns.

In this chapter you will find several original 18th & 19th century powder horns. Information and dimensions are provided for each piece. Studying original powder horns is a great way to get a sense for the artistic style of this unique art form. Learn from these horns, and use them as a reference when making your own. If you are antiquing your horns, study originals to see how they have aged and stressed over time, and mimic it. By adjusting the position of the staple, left hand horns were often made for right hand use.

An original Jacob Dickert long rifle dating from the 1770's. Jacob Dickert immigrated to America from Germany around 1750. He worked in Lancaster County Pennsylvania from 1769, until his death in the early 1820's. Many of his rifles were used by the Continental Army during the American Revolution.

An original Revolutionary War Southern banded horn. Three turned horn rings are heat applied to the body, and attached with wooden pins. The original wooden stopper is still intact.

Bucks County Horn.

A late 18th century Buck's County Pennsylvania powder horn. Measures 13-1/4" long. The lathe turned neck has a threaded head for easy refilling. The base of the horn has a ring overlay made of a separate piece of carved cow horn. The butt plug is turned ash, and retained using iron pins. Two squared iron staples are attached at the butt plug and neck. The left hand side of the horn shows extensive wear at the base and neck. This was caused by the horn rubbing against the owner's body over time, which shows you how much these horns were actually used.

Author's Collection

Original Horns

Lancaster Powder Horn.

A Lancaster factory made powder horn, measuring 11" long. The turned neck is threaded to allow easy refilling. The base of the plug and neck have heat applied collars made from separate pieces of carved horn. The large turned butt plug has decorative carved rings. Two iron staples are attached at the neck and butt for securing a shoulder strap.

Author's Collection

Large Lancaster Powder Horn.

This Lancaster powder horn measures 13-1/2" in length. The turned neck is threaded for easy removal. The threads are still in perfect condition. The base of the neck has an applied collar made from a separate piece of turned horn. The domed butt plug has decorative turned rings, with a large knob for attaching a shoulder strap.

Author's Collection

Recreating the 18th Century Powder Horn

Factory Powder Horn.

A factory made trade powder horn from the early 19th century. This horn measures 10" long, with a turned neck. The butt plug is maple with decorative carving. An iron staple is attached to the neck, angled for right hand use. The base of the horn has a brass drawer pull attached. Drawer pulls were easily purchased, and have been found on many powder horns.

Author's Collection.

An antique brass 'drawer pull'. Shown actual size, these are found on many powder horns of the 18th and 19th centuries. Drawer pulls, staples and screws were easily obtained from local merchants.

Powder Horn with Measure.

This 1780 - 1810 era powder horn measures 11-1/4" in length. The horn has a round neck, with carved ring. The body has a simple scraped finish. The hard wood butt plug is carved flat, and retained by several iron nails. Two brass drawer pulls are attached at the neck and plug for attaching a horn strap. This horn retains its original turned brass powder measure.

Author's Collection.

Original Horns

Indian Trade Horns.
Plain 18th century trade horns. Plain horns were commonly purchased by Native Americans for use with their trade guns. Both horns are 11" in length, with carved necks, and no further embellishments.

Author's Collection.

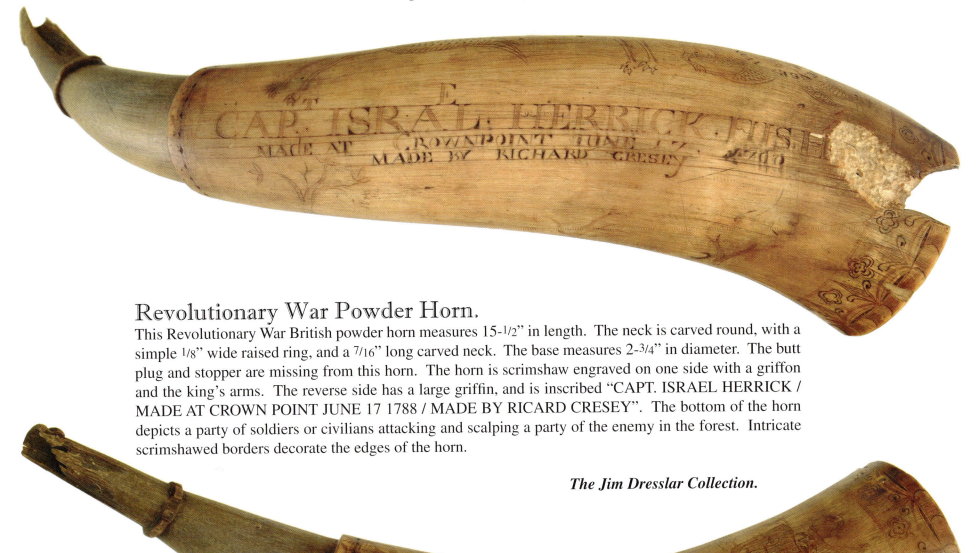

Revolutionary War Powder Horn.

This Revolutionary War British powder horn measures 15-1/2" in length. The neck is carved round, with a simple 1/8" wide raised ring, and a 7/16" long carved neck. The base measures 2-3/4" in diameter. The butt plug and stopper are missing from this horn. The horn is scrimshaw engraved on one side with a griffon and the king's arms. The reverse side has a large griffin, and is inscribed "CAPT. ISRAEL HERRICK / MADE AT CROWN POINT JUNE 17 1788 / MADE BY RICARD CRESEY". The bottom of the horn depicts a party of soldiers or civilians attacking and scalping a party of the enemy in the forest. Intricate scrimshawed borders decorate the edges of the horn.

The Jim Dresslar Collection.

Original Horns

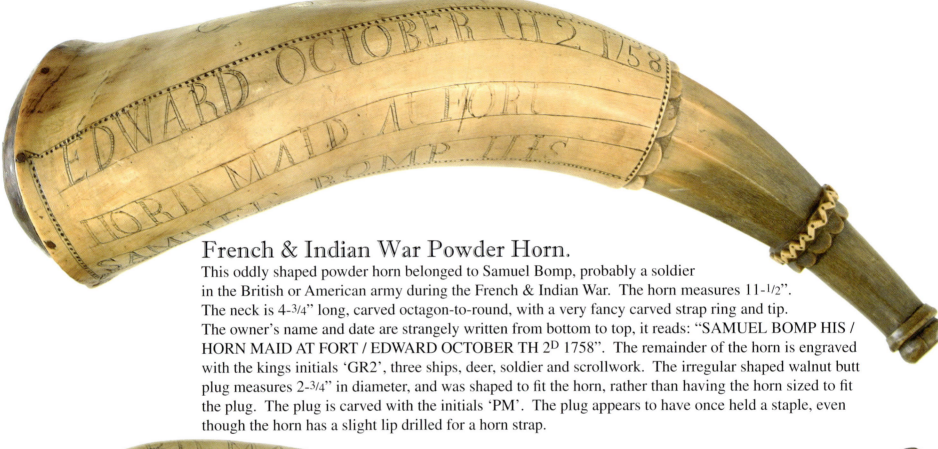

French & Indian War Powder Horn.

This oddly shaped powder horn belonged to Samuel Bomp, probably a soldier in the British or American army during the French & Indian War. The horn measures 11-1/2". The neck is 4-3/4" long, carved octagon-to-round, with a very fancy carved strap ring and tip. The owner's name and date are strangely written from bottom to top, it reads: "SAMUEL BOMP HIS / HORN MAID AT FORT / EDWARD OCTOBER TH 2^D 1758". The remainder of the horn is engraved with the kings initials 'GR2', three ships, deer, soldier and scrollwork. The irregular shaped walnut butt plug measures 2-3/4" in diameter, and was shaped to fit the horn, rather than having the horn sized to fit the plug. The plug is carved with the initials 'PM'. The plug appears to have once held a staple, even though the horn has a slight lip drilled for a horn strap.

The Jim Dresslar Collection.

Original Horns

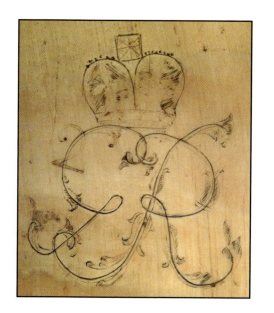

Close up views of the scrimshaw and architecture of the horn neck. Notice the fine details on the ship and initials. The engrailment is composed of fancy petals. The neck is shaped with octagon flats. The fancy strap ring, with a zig-zag pattern, has a matching petal engrailment. The tip is finished round with a raised ring at the spout.

Paneled Powder Horn.

This powder horn measures 10-3/4" with a 2-1/2" wide oval butt plug. This unique horn has three raised panels with decoratively carved borders. The 4" long neck is carved with eight flats, the top flat being engraved with the Freemason's emblem. Two large rings are carved into the neck for a horn strap. The carving at the base of the neck is quite unique, having three layers of engrailing. The domed walnut plug is retained by four wood pins, with a brass staple for attaching a strap.

The Jim Dresslar Collection.

Original Horns

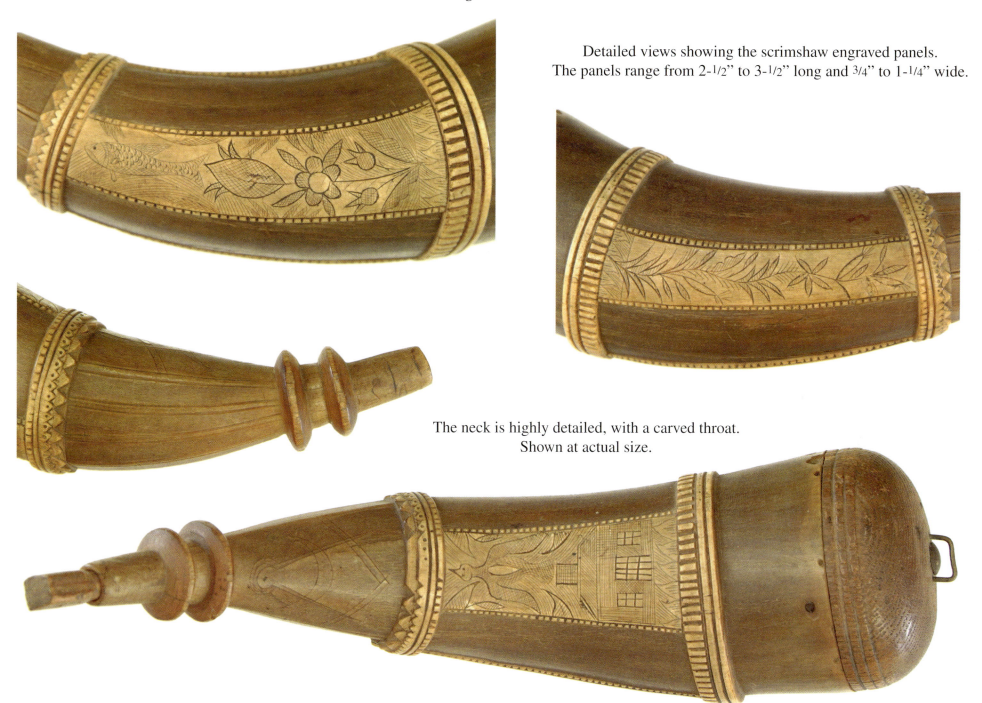

Detailed views showing the scrimshaw engraved panels.
The panels range from 2-1/2" to 3-1/2" long and 3/4" to 1-1/4" wide.

The neck is highly detailed, with a carved throat.
Shown at actual size.

MicMac Indian Powder Horn.

A fine example of a MicMac powder horn. This horn measures 12" with a 2-1/8" diameter flat butt plug, retained by 11 domed brass tacks. The base of the neck is carved with 15 flats, now worn almost round. The neck has a raised strap ring, carved with another 12 flats. The head, probably added later, is made from the tip of a telescoping brass flask head. The adjustable measuring slots are still visible. The body is fully engraved with geometric patterns and double curves, commonly found on MicMac horns. The remnants of a leather shoulder strap are still present.

The Jim Dresslar Collection.

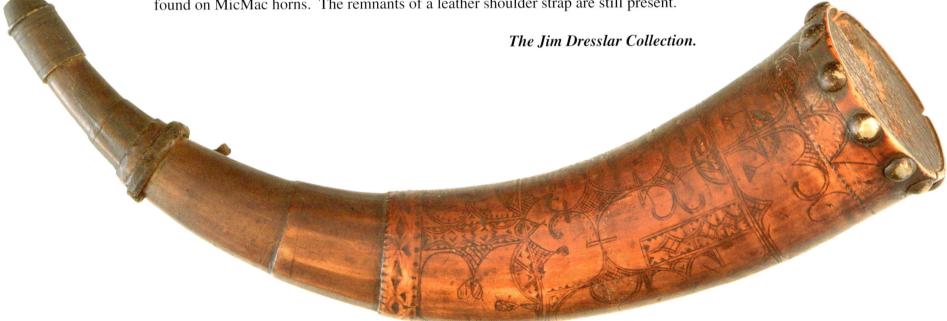

Original Horns

The brass flask head, shown actual size.

Recreating the 18th Century Powder Horn

18th Century British Powder Horn.

This French & Indian War or Revolutionary War horn measures 14" long, with a 4-1/4" long neck. The neck is carved round-to-octagon, with flared grooves, and a 1/2" long raised spout. The body is scrimshaw engraved on the front with the king's arms, griffon, and a mermaid combing her hair. The reverse side shows only an unidentified fortress with blockhouse. The horn has a course woven linen shoulder strap with turned edges, probably a later addition.

The Jim Dresslar Collection.

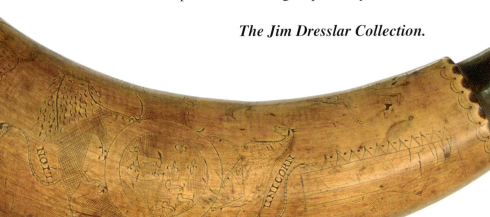

French & Indian War Powder Horn.

A large left hand powder horn measuring 15-1/2". The 6-1/2" long neck is carved with seven flats and an octagonal carved strap ring. The shoulder strap has worn a groove into the neck from years of use. The body is inscribed: "JOHN MILES / HIS HORN / MAY 5TH 1759". The reverse side of the horn has been left undecorated. The domed butt plug measures 3" in diameter, and is made of walnut. Though now mostly worn off, there is evidence that the plug was stained black. The plug is retained by 12 wooden pins, with an iron staple mounted on the base.

The Jim Dresslar Collection.

Recreating the 18th Century Powder Horn

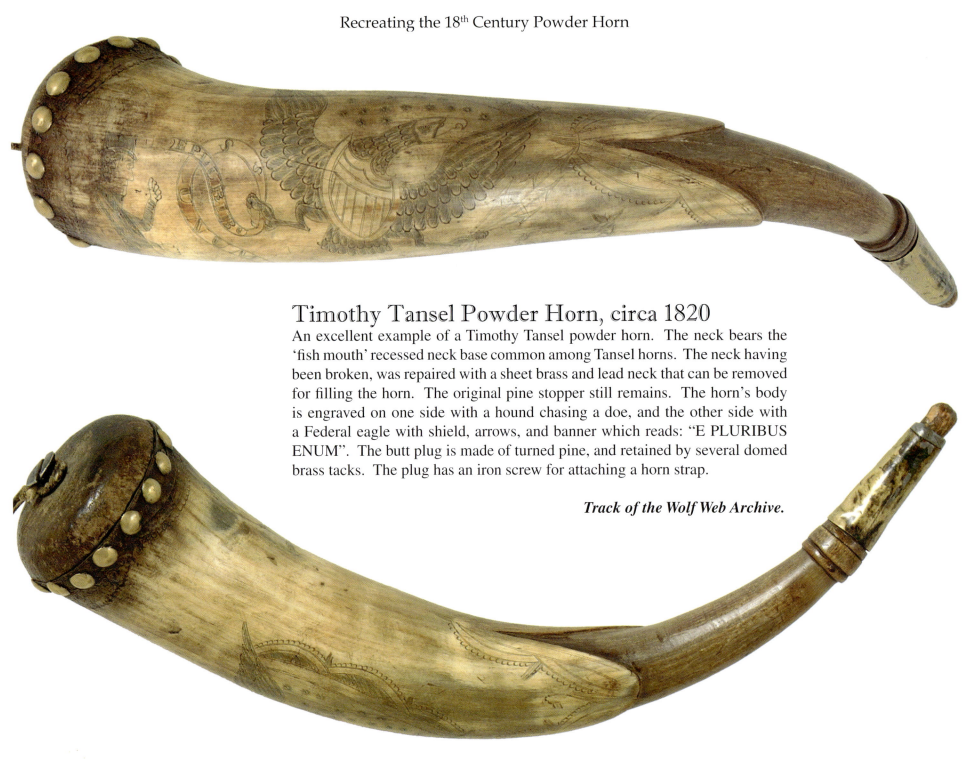

Timothy Tansel Powder Horn, circa 1820

An excellent example of a Timothy Tansel powder horn. The neck bears the 'fish mouth' recessed neck base common among Tansel horns. The neck having been broken, was repaired with a sheet brass and lead neck that can be removed for filling the horn. The original pine stopper still remains. The horn's body is engraved on one side with a hound chasing a doe, and the other side with a Federal eagle with shield, arrows, and banner which reads: "E PLURIBUS ENUM". The butt plug is made of turned pine, and retained by several domed brass tacks. The plug has an iron screw for attaching a horn strap.

Track of the Wolf Web Archive.

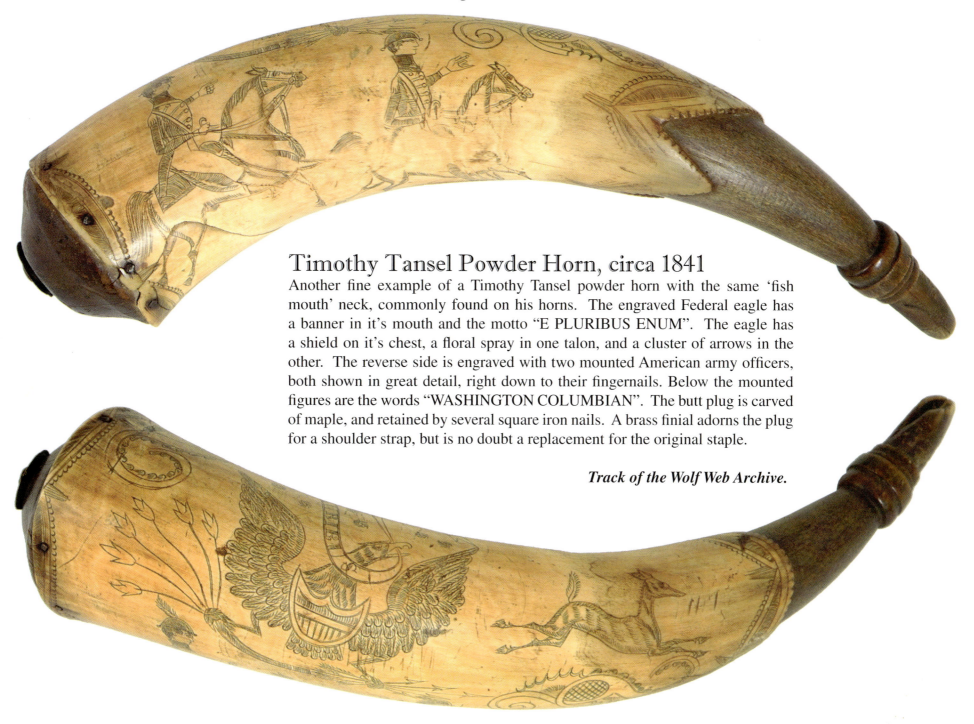

Timothy Tansel Powder Horn, circa 1841

Another fine example of a Timothy Tansel powder horn with the same 'fish mouth' neck, commonly found on his horns. The engraved Federal eagle has a banner in it's mouth and the motto "E PLURIBUS ENUM". The eagle has a shield on it's chest, a floral spray in one talon, and a cluster of arrows in the other. The reverse side is engraved with two mounted American army officers, both shown in great detail, right down to their fingernails. Below the mounted figures are the words "WASHINGTON COLUMBIAN". The butt plug is carved of maple, and retained by several square iron nails. A brass finial adorns the plug for a shoulder strap, but is no doubt a replacement for the original staple.

Track of the Wolf Web Archive.

Reproduction Powder Horns.

This collection of reproduction powder horns by Scott and Cathy Sibley represents only a fraction of those made over the course of two decades. Many are reproductions of originals, and some are their own designs. All were constructed and scrimshaw engraved by Scott and Cathy using the methods shown in this book.

Above: A Long Land pattern "Brown Bess" musket, made by artist Michael Hayes.

Right: Artwork from an original British powder horn from the Jim Dresslar collection.

Below: A reproduction French & Indian War powder horn with a detailed map of Fort Niagara.

Recreating the 18th Century Powder Horn

A Revolutionary War style powder horn with matching scalloped carved rings and neck engrailment. The body is scrimshaw engraved with British soldiers performing a "street firing" exercise. The horn is also decorated with folk art flowers and geometric designs.

Reproduction Powder Horns

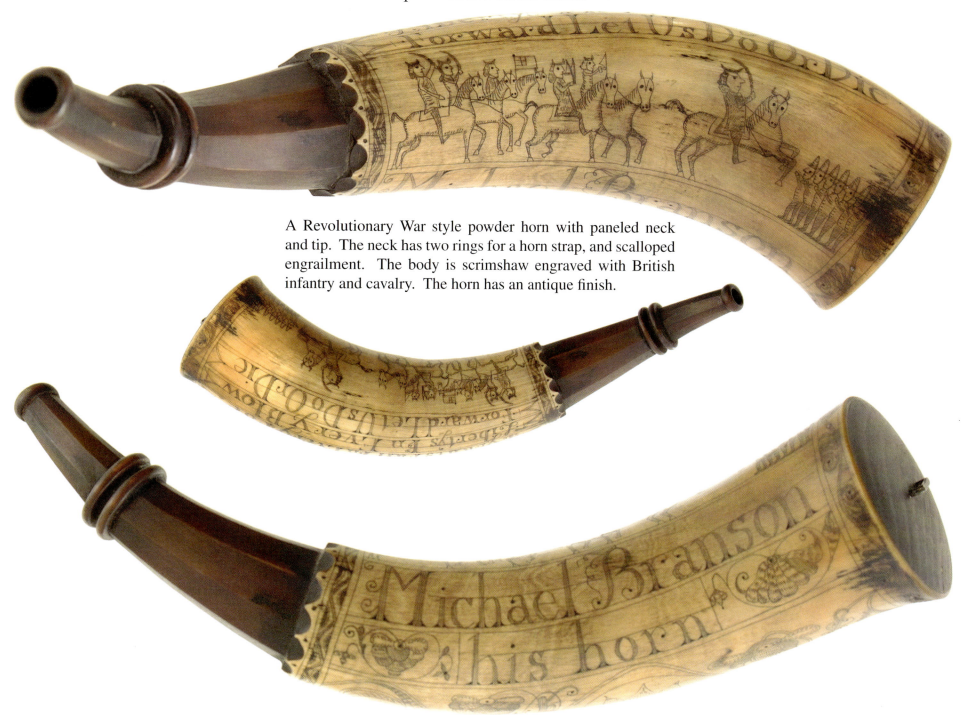

A Revolutionary War style powder horn with paneled neck and tip. The neck has two rings for a horn strap, and scalloped engrailment. The body is scrimshaw engraved with British infantry and cavalry. The horn has an antique finish.

Recreating the 18th Century Powder Horn

An American Revolution patriotic horn with octagon paneled neck. The strap ring is quite large, with a raised ring and scalloped edge. The engrailment on the neck is cut with alternating "U" and "V" gouges. The body is scrimshaw engraved with a detailed map of New York, animals, and patriotic symbols. The flat base of the horn is angle drilled for a horn strap.

Reproduction Powder Horns

A Revolutionary War style powder horn with a fancy tiered panelled neck. Heavily scrimshaw engraved with a map of Lake Ontario and surrounding region. The reverse side bears the kings arms.

Recreating the 18th Century Powder Horn

A Revolutionary War style powder horn with paneled tip, and double strap ring. The octagon-to-round neck has unique engrailment. The base plug is slightly domed with an iron staple.

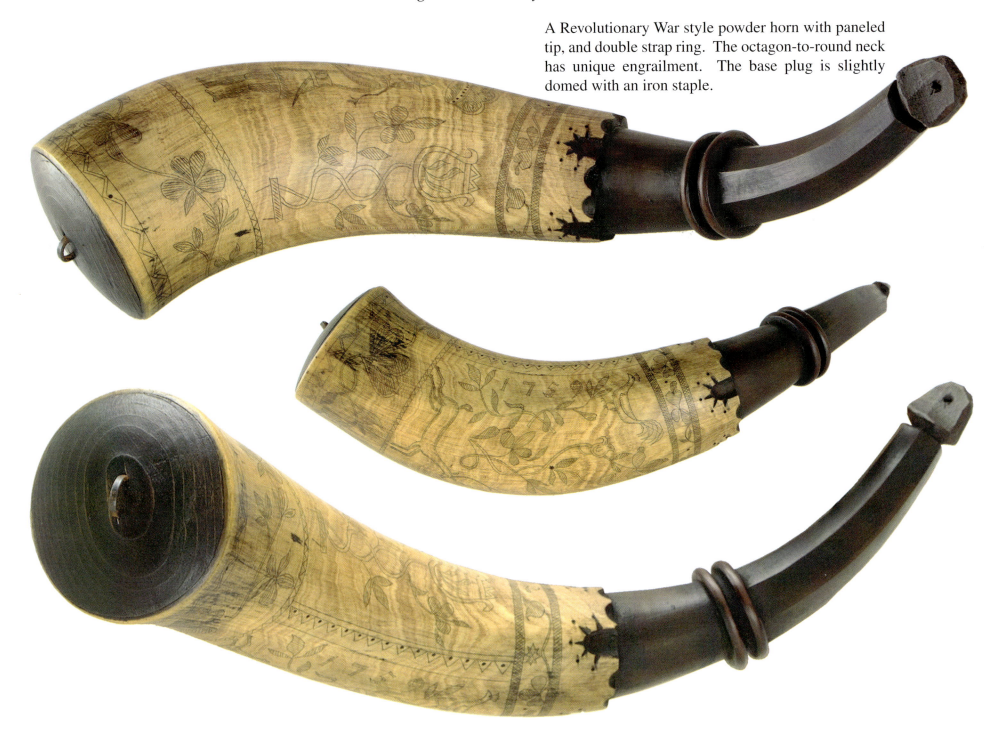

Reproduction Powder Horns

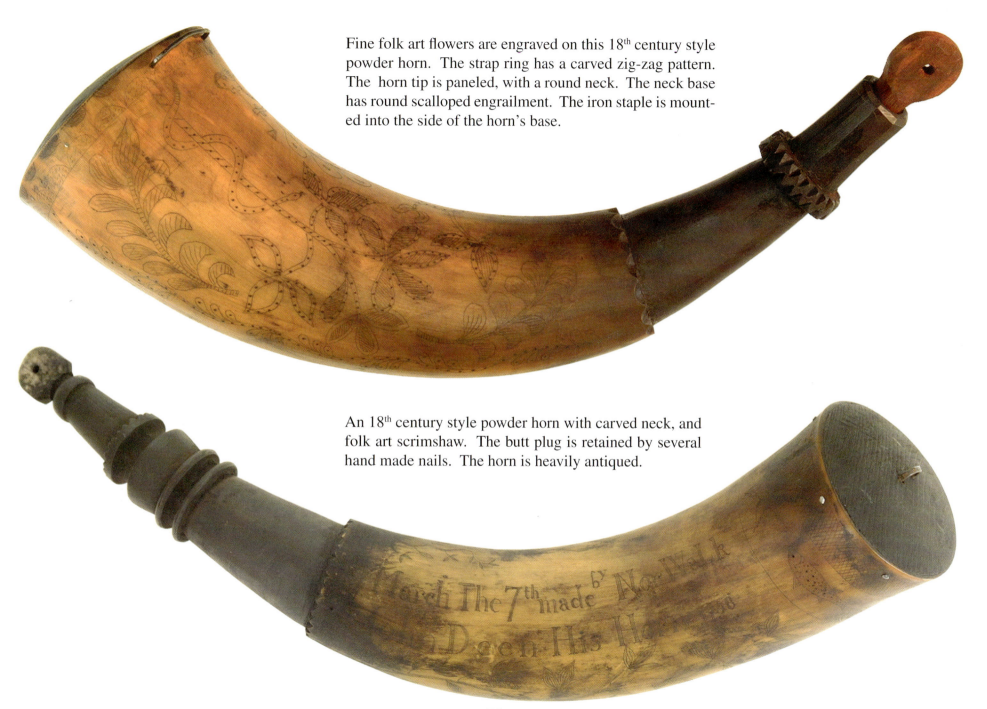

Fine folk art flowers are engraved on this 18th century style powder horn. The strap ring has a carved zig-zag pattern. The horn tip is paneled, with a round neck. The neck base has round scalloped engrailment. The iron staple is mounted into the side of the horn's base.

An 18th century style powder horn with carved neck, and folk art scrimshaw. The butt plug is retained by several hand made nails. The horn is heavily antiqued.

Recreating the 18th Century Powder Horn

A French & Indian War style horn with octagon paneled neck, and green stained plug. The body is heavily scrimshaw engraved with folk art style geometric designs. Note the simple forged iron staples on the butt plug and neck.

Reproduction Powder Horns

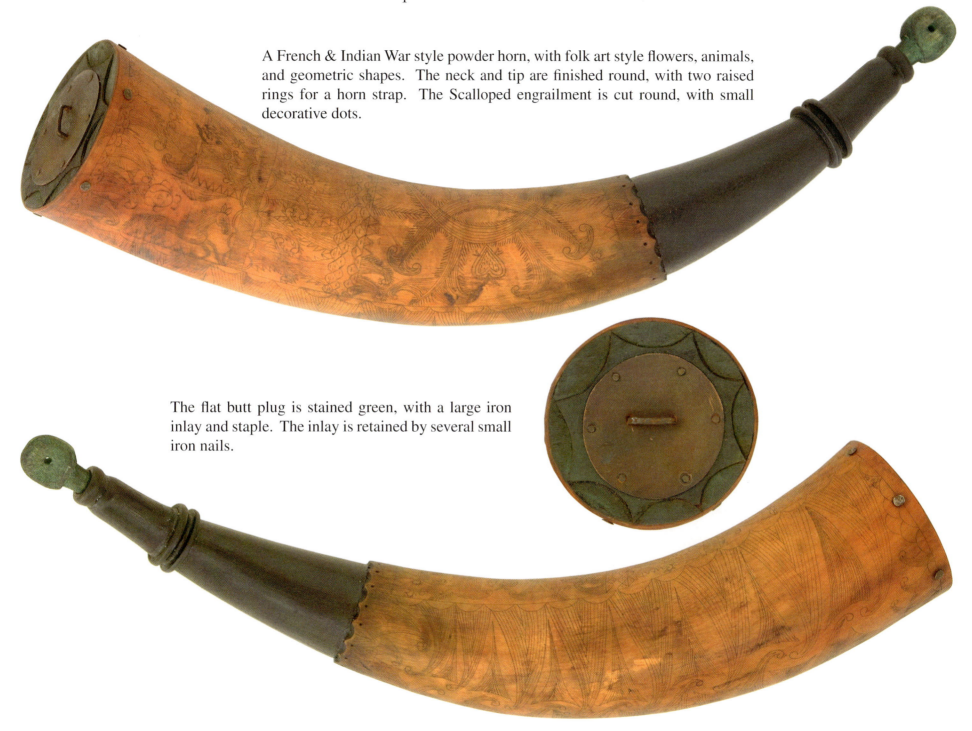

A French & Indian War style powder horn, with folk art style flowers, animals, and geometric shapes. The neck and tip are finished round, with two raised rings for a horn strap. The Scalloped engrailment is cut round, with small decorative dots.

The flat butt plug is stained green, with a large iron inlay and staple. The inlay is retained by several small iron nails.

Recreating the 18th Century Powder Horn

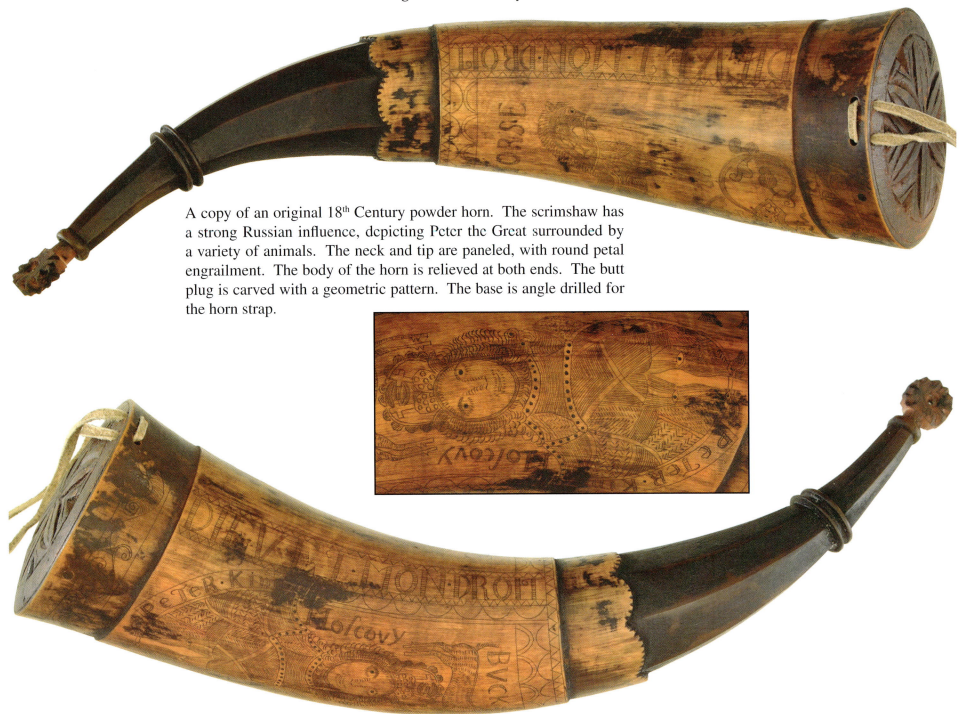

A copy of an original 18th Century powder horn. The scrimshaw has a strong Russian influence, depicting Peter the Great surrounded by a variety of animals. The neck and tip are paneled, with round petal engrailment. The body of the horn is relieved at both ends. The butt plug is carved with a geometric pattern. The base is angle drilled for the horn strap.

Reproduction Powder Horns

A large Revolutionary War style powder horn with a lobed base, popular during the mid 18th century. This horn measures almost twenty inches in length, and is fully scrimshaw engraved.

Recreating the 18th Century Powder Horn

A late 18th century style powder horn, with a Pennsylvania Deutsch theme, and natural color paneled neck. The body of the horn has been relieved, except for two raised rings, and two hearts. The flat horn plug is turned with a button for attaching a horn strap.

Reproduction Powder Horns

A early 19th century style powder horn. This horn has been stained red and heavily antiqued. Rows of domed brass tacks adorn the horn's body and butt plug. The tip is paneled with a raised ring for a horn strap. The horn's neck has been finished into the body with a smooth transition.

A 1770's style Southern ringed horn, with a turned neck and butt plug. The base plug is hollowed to increase the volume of the horn. The horn has three heat applied rings made of turned horn, and held in place with several small metal pins.

Recreating the 18th Century Powder Horn

A dark Southern ringed horn with a turned head of deer antler. The head unscrews for easy refilling. The round domed butt plug is turned maple, rather than the softer pine. The body has two heat applied horn rings.

Another Southern ringed horn, with heat applied horn rings, and a turned "beehive" style butt plug. The turned plug is hollowed to increase the volume of the horn. This horn has been decorated with small burn marks.

Reproduction Powder Horns

Top: A Federal Timothy Tansel style horn with fish mouth engrailment, removable neck, and turned base plug.

Bottom: A large paneled horn, measuring 14-1/2" long with a carved neck. The beehive style plug is 3-1/4" in diameter, tapering to 1-3/4", and is 2" long with 12 individual turned rings.

Recreating the 18th Century Powder Horn

Two 18th century style paneled horns. Notice how the panels flow with the natural shape of the horn. The bottom horn has a raised paneled neck, and scalloped horn ring. The raw horn must have a fairly thick base to allow for the panel shaping.

Reproduction Powder Horns

Based on two Revolutionary War era horns belonging to American militiamen, this horn measures 18-1/2" in length. The base plug is made of turned walnut, with a large turned horn base ring. A glass plate is inset into the plug displaying a hand written note. This style of horn was very rare. The name of the horn's owner was often written here, or some type of drawing was displayed.

Recreating the 18th Century Powder Horn

An 18th century style paneled horn with turned beehive butt plug. The turned plug is hollowed to increase the volume of the horn. Mounted with brass tacks, an iron staple is inset for a horn strap. Panels from the neck an tip flow together, interrupted only by the two raised rings for the horn strap.

Reproduction Powder Horns

A red dyed panel horn with two raised neck rings. The turned walnut butt plug is retained by forged iron nails. The body has an antique finish.

Scrimshaw Designs

ABCDEFGHIJKLMN
OPQRSTUVWXYZ

0123456789
0123456789

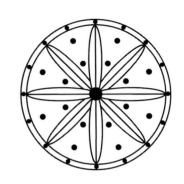

In this last chapter you will find a collection of scrimshaw art, reproduced from original 18th and 19th century powder horns.

Floral & Geometric Designs.

References.

Here you will find a list of reference books and websites showcasing original powder horns. These horns are a great source for ideas and inspiration.

The Engraved Powder Horn
Folk Art of Early America
By Jim Dresslar
Dresslar Publishing Co.
ISBN 0-9651039-0-0

Drums A'Beating, Trumpets Sounding
Artistically Carved Powder Horns in the provincial manner 1746-1781
By William H. Guthman
ISBN 1-881264-05-X

Powder Horns and Their Architecture
By Madison Grant
LCCN# 87-090760

Accouterments, Volumes I, II, & III
By James R. Johnston

Collector's Illustrated Encyclopedia of the American Revolution
By George C. Neumann and Frank J. Kravic
ISBN 0-9605666-8-6

Track of the Wolf Online Historical Archive
http://www.trackofthewolf.com

Photos courtesy of Jim Dresslar.

X-Acto® is a registered trademark of: HUNT X-ACTO, INC. CO. PENNSYLVANIA. 1405 LOCUST ST. PHILADELPHIA, PA 19102

RIT® is a registered trademark of: PHOENIX BRANDS LLC F/K/A WINTER HOLDINGS LLC LIMITED LIABILITY CO. DELAWARE. 399 PARK AVENUE, 9TH FLOOR, NEW YORK, NY 10022

Zip Guard® is a registered trademark of: STAR BRONZE COMPANY CO. OHIO. 803 SOUTH MAHONING AVENUE, ALLIANCE, OH 44601

Vise-Grip® is a registered trademark of: PETERSEN MANUFACTURING COMPANY INCORPORATION NEBRASKA. DEWITT, NE 68341